A
BALTHUS
NOTEBOOK

A
BALTHUS
NOTEBOOK

GUY DAVENPORT

THE ECCO PRESS
New York

The Ecco Press
26 West 17th Street
New York, NY 10011
Published simultaneously in Canada by
Penguin Books Canada Ltd., Ontario
Printed in the United States of America
Designed by Nicola Mazzella
FIRST EDITION

Permission to reproduce the works of Balthus here has been kindly granted on behalf of the artist by the Artists Rights Society, as exclusive agent for SPADEM in the United States. *Copyright 1989 ARS N.Y. / SPADEM.*

Library of Congress Cataloging-in-Publication Data

Davenport, Guy.
  A Balthus notebook / Guy Davenport.
—1st. ed.   p.   cm.
  1. Balthus, 1908- —Criticism and interpretation.   I. Title.
N6853.B3D38 1989   760'.092—dc20   89-36117

ISBN 0-88001-234-X

The text of this book is set in Palatino.

List of Illustrations

1. *The Street*. 1933.
   Oil on canvas, 76 ³/₄ × 94 ¹/₂ in.
   The Museum of Modern Art, New York.
   James Thrall Soby Bequest.

2. *Joan Miró and His Daughter Delores*. 1933-38.
   Oil on canvas, 51 ¹/₄ × 35 in.
   The Museum of Modern Art, New York.
   Abby Aldrich Rockefeller Fund.

3. *André Derain*. 1936.
   Oil on wood, 44 ³/₈ × 28 ¹/₂ in.
   The Museum of Modern Art, New York.
   Acquired through the Lillie P. Bliss Bequest.

4. *The Passage du Commerce Saint-André*. 1952-54.
   Oil on canvas, 115 × 130 in.
   Courtesy Musée National d'Art Moderne, Paris.
   Private Collection.

5. *The Children*. 1937.
   Oil on canvas, 49 ¹/₄ × 50 ³/₄ in.
   Musée du Louvre, Paris. Donation Pablo Picasso.
   Copyright © PHOTO R.M.N. - SPADEM.

6. *The Painter and His Model*. 1981.
   Casein tempera on canvas, 89 $^1/_4$ × 91 $^3/_4$ in.
   Collection, Musée National d'Art Moderne, Paris.

7. *The Golden Days*. 1944-46.
   Oil on canvas, 58 $^1/_4$ × 78 $^3/_8$ in.
   The Hirshhorn Museum and Sculpture Garden,
   Smithsonian Institution, Washington, D.C.
   Gift of Joseph H. Hirshhorn, 1966.

1

IF THERE are eternal values in art, it seems they are preserved only by those who strive to realize them in a new content (Schapiro, 168).

2

CULTURE IS not merely juxtaposed to life nor superimposed upon it, but in one way serves as a substitute for life, and in the other, uses it and transforms it, to bring about the synthesis of a new order (Lévi-Strauss 1969, 4).

3

If, as Robert Walser remarked, God is the opposite of Rodin, Balthus is the opposite of Picasso.

Mondriaan, of Brancusi, "Ah! That great realist."

5

THE REPROACH of escapism is seldom aimed at a painter; we do not hold it against Cézanne that he was living hidden away at Estaque during the war of 1870. And we recall with respect his *"C'est effrayant, la vie,"* even when the lowliest student, ever since Nietzsche, would flatly reject philosophy if it did not teach him how to live fully (*à être de grands vivants*).

It is as if in the painter's calling there were some urgency above all other claims on him. Strong or frail in life, he is incontestably sovereign in his own rumination of the world. With no other technique than what his eyes and hands discover in seeing and painting, he persists in drawing from this world, with its din of history's glories and scandals, *canvases* which will hardly add to the angers or hopes of man—and no one complains.

What, then, is this secret science which he has or which he seeks? That dimension which lets van Gogh say he must go "further on"? What is this fundamental of painting, perhaps of all culture? (Merleau-Ponty, 161)

BALTHUS'S *Mitsou: Quarante images par Baltusz, préface de Rainer Maria Rilke* (Zürich and Leipzig, 1921), was published a year before Janusc Korczak's *Krol Macius Pierwszy* (Warsaw, 1922). Balthus was thirteen, Korczak forty-four. Balthus had already done illustrations "for a Chinese novel" (Rewald, 167), and between 1932 and 1934 he would do a suite of drawings to illustrate *Wuthering Heights* (eight of these appeared in the surrealist magazine *Minotaure*, no. 7, 1935, and all of them are reproduced in Rewald, 161–166).

The conjunction of *Mitsou* and *King Matt the First* is on a ground of a new responsibility and autonomy for children laid down in a diverse but coherent way by the Wandervögel in Germany and Scandinavia, Baron de Coubertin in France (and this would lead to the modern Olympics, though Coubertin's plan to include children would be thwarted), the Boy Scouts and Girl Guides in England and the United States (absorbing Ernest Thompson Seton's Woodcraft Indians movement); by Kipling in *Kim* and *The Jungle Books;* by Edgar Rice Burroughs (Tarzan was an adolescent when he became ruler of a forest kingdom); and by other forces moving children from their status as "the world's largest proletariat," as Korczak said when he undertook to be their Karl Marx.

Mitsou is only tangentially within this movement, but it is a book by a child, a category of which the world had hitherto been whimsically tolerant, and it is in the manner of Frans Masereel, the Belgian pacifist, exile (in Switzerland), and friend of Balthus's mother, Baladine Klossowska. Masereel invented the novel without a text, using Expressionist woodcuts instead. His first imitator is Balthus, his second Max Ernst in *La femme 100 têtes* (1929) and *Une semaine de bonté* (1933). This invention is actually a restitution of preliterate narrative art, as in church carvings and windows, the medieval woodcut, and prints in series, such as Hogarth's *Marriage à la Mode* and *The Rake's Progress.* The influence on Balthus of Hogarth is extensive and deep.

The forty drawings in *Mitsou* tell of a little boy (Balthus himself, as we can see from photographs) who finds a cat on a park bench, appropriates it, has many domestic adventures with it, and eventually suffers its disappearance. It is a love story with an unhappy ending. We can see in it the creation of a persistent symbol: the cat becomes Balthus's daimon as well as his alter ego. It is his representative in many paintings of day-dreaming girls. It is his symbol of the animal in our nature. The cat is a sensual, cunning, sly, rapacious creature, easily tamed but never giving up its wildness, to which it reverts in fear, territorial wars, and mating.

Balthus painted himself once as a cat dining on fish, and once as the King of the Cats.

"In 1922, when he was fourteen," Sabine Rewald begins her book about him, "Balthus told a friend that he wanted to remain a child forever."

Korczak's *King Matt the First*, a masterpiece of children's literature in our century, has the power of *Candide* in its ironic bite and the charm that Antoine de Saint-Éxupéry would later achieve in *Le petit prince* (1943). It is also a book that was used in Korczak's orphanage in Warsaw as a cult text. In fact, it was written for the orphans. The story is of a ten-year-old king who rules with genius. He has the diamond-cutting rationality of Voltaire, Washington's nobility, and a mischievous touch of Tom Sawyer playing a king. His programs of reform reach their limit when he attempts to make a social class of children and urge them to revolt against grown-ups all over the world.

This, whether intentionally or not, was Fourier's vision of a New Harmony, principally designed for children, with a ten-year-old king as the final authority in the governance of all the world's phalansteries.

Pierre Klossowski, Balthus's novelist brother, tells us that Walter Benjamin's Marxism "was intent on safeguarding, in his vast erudition (conforming to a thoroughly lyrical sensibility), what in the past had constituted for [Benjamin] the 'shadow of the goods to come.' Among these goods to come figured the vision of a society blossoming in the *free play of the passions*. His nostalgia aspired to reconcile Marx and Fourier" (Smith, 368).

In a stratification that zones off children from adults (reminiscent of Rousseau's distinction between noble savagery and civilization) and assigns a native creativity and intelligence, along with a radical innocence, to children, we can place Balthus, who wanted to remain a child all his life, and who chose to meditate in so many canvases on the passage at puberty from child to adult. In *Mitsou* he meditates on the child's experience of loss, folding in two symbols that would remain with him, the lively Mitsou of Colette and her loss (causing Proust to cry) and Mitsou the independent cat, which, having accepted Balthus's love and protection, simply walked away.

He sits, that cat, in canvas after canvas, playing Puck and commenting on what fools these mortals be, playing Balthus the grown-up, playing the Cheshire cat grinning in Olympian apathy.

One way of looking at Balthus is to see all the paintings as a complex *Mitsou* in which Colette's spritely girl has displaced her namesake cat, in which the form is now symphonic and rich in variations, with resonant quotations from Hogarth, Emily Brontë, Rilke, Courbet. A culture, Ruskin said, must be judged according to how it treats its children.

Balthus is well aware that we inhabit a world in

which, on August 6, 1942, Korczak's Republic of Children, 192 of them, were marched by the Gestapo from the Warsaw ghetto to a train that took them to Treblinka, where, that afternoon, they were all gassed with the exhaust from trucks. Korczak led the procession, carrying a five-year-old girl named Romcia and holding the hand of another child, Szymonek Jakubowicz. At the end of the double file was a fifteen-year-old boy carrying the flag of King Matt, a Star of David on a white field (Lifton, 340).

In 1942 Balthus, a Jew by the Gestapo's reckoning (Rewald, 11), was painting meadows in the Rhone Valley, patient oxen, and children playing a card game called patience.

7

"Mɪᴛsᴏᴜ ɪs resting, alone. She is wearing strawberry coloured stockings sewn on to her tights by the tops, a pair of gilt shoes and a mauve crepon kimono. Nature has given Mitsou all the advantages that fashion is demanding: very small nose, large eyes as black as her hair, round cheeks, a small, sulky, fresh mouth—that is her face. For the figure what is required is a slender body with long and well-shaped legs, and small and low-slung breasts; well, she has all that with only the small defect of a slight skinniness about the knee. But the thirties will fill up those page-boy's thighs, and also the back that is like an anaemic nymph's; Mitsou is only twenty-four.

"Mitsou is alone, sitting at her dressing table. Her legs, opened in a V, are held stiff so as not to strain her stockings, but her young back bends and her neck falls forward, as if she were a thirsty gazelle" (Colette, 341–342).

Colette's first description of Mitsou in *Mitsou ou Comment l'esprit vient aux filles* (1913).

8

BALTHUS'S ADOLESCENTS have a history. The Enlightenment, removing encrustations of convention from human nature, discovered the *durée* of childhood as the most passionate and beautiful part of a lifetime. (In Plutarch's *Lives,* no childhoods are recorded.) Rousseau, Blake, Joshua Reynolds, Gainsborough, Wordsworth.

By the Belle Époque, children (in a pervasive, invisible revolution) had come into a world of their own for the first time in Western civilization since late antiquity, and we begin to have (in Proust, in Joyce) dramatic accounts of their world as never before. Henry James's "The Turn of the Screw" (which now that we have Balthus seems Balthusian) is a skirmish on the border between the inner worlds of child and adult. James follows with symbols the serious misunderstanding between the interiority of the two realms.

It is significant that anthropologists around this time, inspecting other cultures, thought of themselves as studying "the childhood of mankind." Balthus is a contemporary of Gide and Henry de Montherlant, who, like Fourier and Wordsworth, were trying to *place* the child's random vitality. Balthus's adolescents, in an endless afternoon of reading, playing cards, and daydreaming, seem to have come, we are told, as a subject for inexhaustible meditation from *Wuthering*

Heights, a dismal and hysterical novel that he reads in his own way.

What caught Balthus's imagination in it was the manner in which children create a subsidiary world, an emotional island which they have the talent to *robin-soner,* to fill all the contours of. This subworld has its own time, its own weather, its own customs and morals. The only clock I can find in Balthus is on the mantel of *The Golden Days* in the Hirshhorn, and its dial is out of the picture.

Balthus's children have no past (childhood resorbs a memory that cannot yet be consulted) and no future (as a concern). They are outside time.

9

MODERN FRENCH writing has been interested in childhood and adolescence in a way that American and English writing have not. The French see an innocent but an experienced mind in the child. Montherlant treats children as an endangered species needing protection from parents. Gide's understanding runs parallel, except that he makes allowance for the transformation to maturity. The child in Alain-Fournier, Colette, Cocteau inhabits a realm imaginatively animated with a genius very like that of the artist. Children live in their minds.

Baudelaire saw genius as childhood sustained and perfected. There is a sense among the French that adulthood is a falling away from the intelligence of children. We in the United States contrast child and adult as we contrast ignorance and knowledge, innocence and experience.

We do not give our children credit for having arrived at anything. They have no driver's license, no money, no sexual emotions (and are forbidden them), no real sports they can play, no power. Balthus's children are as complacent as cats and as accomplished in stillness.

We have postponed fulfillment of heart and mind far too late, so that the spiritual rhythm, or bad habit, of American children is perpetual procrastination.

American writing and art make the child an actor in an adult world (Mark Twain, Salinger), not a real being in its own.

Of the autistically interior, dreaming, reading, erotic, self-sufficient child in Balthus's painting we have practically no image at all. Balthus's children are not being driven to succeed where their parents failed, or to be popular, adjusted, and addicted to acquisitiveness.

CHILDREN ARE the creatures of their culture. The nakedness of human nature is clothed so soon by every culture that we are at a wide variance, within and among cultures, as to what human nature might be. It was one of the hopes of our century to find out, a hope wholly dashed.

In France this question was thoroughly and originally debated during the Enlightenment and Revolution. The building facing us in *The Passage du Commerce Saint-André* was Marat's newspaper office; the neighborhood once saw the movements of David and Diderot.

Charles Fourier (1772–1837) concocted an elaborate philosophy to discover human nature and invented a utopian society to accommodate it, a society of children organized into hives and roving bands. Adults were, so to speak, to be recruited from the ranks of this aristocracy.

Proust's "little band" of adolescent girls at Balbec derives from Fourier, and the narrator's male presence among them is according to Fourier's plan of organization. Saint-Loup and his circle constitute a Little Horde, the complement of "Spartans" to the Athenian Little Bands.

11

BALTHUS'S EROTIC sense disarms because of its literalness, explicitness, and evasion of vulgarity or cheapness of any sort. He brings the taste of Fragonard and Watteau into our century, where it is unlikely to survive except in Balthus's careful, protective sensibility. Watteau's ladies and milkmaids know that we are looking at them, and are forever beyond us in an imaginary world. Balthus's girls with bared crotches are usually looking at themselves, in a brown study or reverie, provocative, vulnerable, neither innocent nor naive.

The girl in *The Golden Days* is looking at her fetching self in a hand mirror and is sitting so that that young man feeding the fire will see her underwear, if any, when he turns. We see instead slim and charming adolescence trying on an expression for effect.

12

THE TERM "modern artist" has never had a strictly temporal sense; from the beginning it has designated a totemistic clan to which one belongs according to a structure of rules with tribal overtones as yet to be described. Balthus is as yet a provisionally kin country cousin. Sir Herbert Read, for instance, decreed that Stanley Spencer was not a modern artist. We remember that Brancusi, to please a committee, had to redraw a portrait of Joyce because it wasn't modern enough for their taste.

Balthus, I suspect, has been excluded from the clan for reasons of awesome primitiveness, and has thus remained in the distinguished category of the unclassifiable, like Wyndham Lewis and Stanley Spencer. If modernity ended by trivializing its revolution (conspicuous novelty displacing creativity), it also has a new life awaiting it in a retrospective survey of what it failed to include in its sense of itself.

13

BALTHUS AND Spencer illuminate each other. Spencer's intrepid religious grounding (eccentric, Blakean, British, Bunyanesque; the naive inextricably in harmony with the sophisticated elements) is like Balthus's privileged, undisclosed, but articulate psychology. Both painters express a sensual delight in the material world that is openly hedonistic, an accomplishment of their imaginations beyond the sensitivity of criticism: the way light rakes a brick wall in Spencer, the respect for carpentry and architecture in Balthus.

Both Balthus and Spencer give us the surface of the canvas as a mimesis of natural textures, not paint. In Picasso, van Gogh, on out to the reductio ad absurdum of Pollock, it is paint. The difference is a philosophical one, perhaps even a religious one.

Spencer's iconography of saws, ironwork, human flesh reseen without the authority of neoclassical conventions, kettles, drying laundry, the location of shadows in naked light parallels Balthus's return to a realism of an accomplished eye that demands accuracy of detail and that generalizes nothing.

14

WE HAVE yet to study in modern painting the choice of motif after the break between patron and artist in the early nineteenth century. Not even the portrait as a document or landscape as a sentiment for a room's decoration survives this new context for the visual arts. This change was also a metamorphosis in taste. Malraux has his theory: that art became an absolute, that from Goya forward painting had only its authority as a witness to proceed with, alienated in one sense (from church and palace) but liberated in another to its own destiny.

15

Where in Greek writing you always find a running account of all the senses in intimate contact with the world, in Latin you find instead a pedantry accustomed to substituting some rhetorical convention for honest and immediate perception. Balthus has Greek wholeness. Nietzsche says somewhere that the Greek love of adolescents arose from the value they placed on their achievement as a people. The French woman, as a cultural type, recognizes her adolescence in Balthus's girls.

16

BALTHUS HAS the immediacy of a naive painter. Picasso's figures are all actors, wearers of masks, mediators, like Picasso himself, between reality and illusion. Pierrot, woman as artist's model, the Ballet Russe, the commedia dell'arte dominate his entire oeuvre. Nowhere in Balthus does this theme of actor and theater appear (though he has designed for the stage and was a friend of Artaud). There is great integrity in his resisting it. His tradition stands apart from that of Rouault, Braque, Picasso, Klee, Ensor, and others for whom acting has been a metaphor and art a stage.

Nor do we find in Balthus any overt enlistment of mythology, which has been so characteristic of his time. No Venuses, no Danaës among all those girls. Even his cats and gnomes do not derive from folklore or myth. He is not part of any renaissance. His work is an invention.

Each painting is an invention, not the application of a technique. Each painting holds an imaginary conversation with some other painter, *The Window* with Bonnard, *The Farmyard* with Cézanne, *The Living Room* with Courbet, *The Dream* with Chardin.

The Mountain (in which the girl in the foreground stretches with the feline inflection of Gregor Samsa's sister at the end of "The Metamorphosis") is a dialogue with the Courbet of *Les rochers de Mouthiers* and *La falaise d'Étretat après l'orage.*

THESE CONVERSATIONS among painters can be three-way, and complex. In *Nude with Cat and Mirror* (1977–1980) the girl is from Simone Martini, and the cat, exactly quoted, is from Hogarth's *The Graham Children,* an engaging painting in which a boy, entertaining his three sisters, thinks he is making a caged canary flutter by playing a music box, whereas the bird is fluttering because the family cat is staring at it and trying to mesmerize it. Is the cat in Balthus seeing itself in the girl's mirror? Balthus's painting is about virginity and desire, as all its iconography attests: bed, nudity, billet-doux, the brazier, the mirror, the transfixed cat. In both paintings the cat absorbs all the evil, leaving innocence to fill the rest of the space. A close study of Hogarth and Balthus will turn up many affinities.

18

In *The Visit* (1939), a Surrealist painting by Paul Delvaux, we see a bare room in which a naked woman is
sitting on a wicker-seated stool. Her hair is done in the
style of a Victorian (or Roman) matron. She is cupping
her hands under her breasts, as if to offer them to a
sucking infant. Before her is a naked boy who is enter-
ing the room through a wooden door (scarcely match-
ing the room's decorated ceiling and chandelier) that
opens directly onto a cobblestone-paved street. The
painting can be only of a dream, as the boy would not
have been naked on the street, the door belongs to a
humbler house, and the occasion for the boy's visit
must be looked for in the realm of fantasy and must be
generated by some anxiety about nudity, children, and
adults.

Alex Comfort remarks in *Darwin and the Naked Lady:
Discursive Essays on Biology and Art* that Delvaux is, among
other things, showing us how our response to the
painting is a matter of cultural rules. If the boy had
wings, he would be Cupid, the woman would be
Venus, and the painting would be a trite recycling of a
classical theme.

Dr. Comfort does not go on to notice angels with
trumpets painted on the Baroque ceiling (traditional
accompaniments of Virgin and Child), or count the

candles in the chandelier (six, the number on the altar). In most Madonnas Jesus is naked to signify that he is without original sin, clothing being necessary only after the Fall.

Deviations from iconographic convention register as a transgression and take their meaning from the transgression, as with Max Ernst's *The Blessed Virgin Chastising the Child Jesus Before Three Witnesses.*

Delvaux, whatever else he is doing in *The Visit,* is refilling the emptiness of drained symbols. Balthus is everywhere concerned with returning to subjects of perennial interest that have lost their immediacy and along with it their meaning.

Meaning is always of a wholeness. When Delacroix and Ingres painted odalisques, the harem constituted a critique of the body, its governance, the sources of power over it. An odalisque by Matisse is simply a model in a chair. From slaves and wage slaves to Balthus is the distance between slavery and liberty.

19

Meadow, farm, field, country town—Balthus's landscapes are a return to Pissarro, to take up where he left off. Balthus is interested in the same continuities as in his interiors: the survival of certain manners, ways of spending time, intimacies of the bath and bed. Impressionism was devoted to roads, paths, rivers: a collective study of the network of roads that connected one French village to another. These ways were once ancient sheep paths, then market roads, then the highway system of the Romans. Impressionism was an assessment of civilization up to its time, as if prophetically aware that in 1914–1918 all this would be mud and trenches; seventy French cathedrals would collapse under artillery fire; a mode of life would be forever lost. *Swann's Way* (the name of a road) ends with automobiles in the Bois de Boulogne.

Cubism moved indoors, focusing on the humblest tabletops. Impressionism followed its logical study in Monet, back to the roadless France of prehistory—to the marshlands before they were drained for agriculture. That's what the lily pond at Giverny is, and the haystacks (winter fodder) are almost as archaic. But the beginning was with Pissarro's farms, fields, orchards; fields measured out in baronial times, apple orchards as old as Gaul (apples came north with the Romans, as did the pear, Roman wheat, Latin, the engineering of canals and bridges, walled cities, strange Mediterranean gods).

So Balthus when he turned to landscape emphasized local geography, the specific character of particular places, generalizing nothing. As his houses are without electricity, without radios, TV, telephones; without bathtubs or faucets; his farms are eighteenth-century, using horse and ox power. The figures in his landscapes wave greetings. Van Gogh had painted farmers as drudges and starving peasants. Balthus's farms are visions of pastoral life.

Stephen Dobyns in his *The Balthus Poems* (in which he writes poems about thirty-two of the paintings) catches the tone of Balthusian pastoral in "Landscape with Oxen":

> *With the boards he will build a shelter for spring lambs*
> *that he will fatten in summer, sell in the fall, and*
> *of this pattern of seasonal routine he has woven a life*
> *much in the way his wife weaves the wool into thick cloth,*
> *into such a blue jacket as the farmer is now wearing,*
> *which the lawless wind tries uselessly to take from him.*
>
> (Dobyns, 34)

20

BALTHUS'S TREATMENT of the human figure ranges from a *gaucherie* thoroughly primitive (crones, the boy with pigeons, that cat) to a sensuality and accuracy that put him among the master draftsmen. He paints from inside the figure outward, as if the figure painted itself.

21

THE PSYCHOLOGICAL acumen of the portraits of Derain and Miró is Shakespearean: speaking portraits in the common lore of what a portrait should be. They are, in a disturbing sense, too lifelike. And they are not here as painters primarily, but as the fathers of daughters. They are soliloquies in paint. (Chagall, around the time of the Derain and Miró portraits, had himself photographed with his deliciously sexy twelve-year-old daughter wholly naked, achieving an homage to and subtle parody of Balthus, but recognizing his authority of innovation and iconology.)

22

THE PORTRAIT of the Vicomtesse de Noailles (1936), curiously like Wyndham Lewis's portrait of Edith Sitwell, is beguiling because of its honest, unflattering likeness and unconventionality of pose: a third-grade schoolteacher, surely, resting between classes. This portrait illustrates as well as any of Balthus's his ability to take the bare minimum of a subject and bring it to the highest pitch of clarity, of presence. This rich spareness contrasts with the century's aesthetic of merging figure and ground in a dazzle.

23

The Passage du Commerce Saint-André, Balthus's master-work, has the spaciousness and presence of a Renaissance wall painting (it is eleven feet long, ten feet high) and invites and defies a reading of its meaning as vigorously as Piero della Francesca's *Flagellation.* Reproductions of it trick one into believing that it is an intimist canvas, fairly small. I was unprepared for its size when I saw it first at the Centre Pompidou in an afternoon of surprises. I had just seen my first Tatlin and some late Maleviches unknown until then. I had seen an abstraction by Ivan Puni that made me feel for the moment that Western design still had everything to learn all over again from the Russians.

The surprise of suddenly turning and gazing into (not at) Balthus's great painting was a splendid and complex experience.

For the first time I remembered how familiar the street was to me, a locale I crossed time and again when I first knew Paris just after the war. The painting did not exist then, though Balthus must have been making studies of it, a picture to epitomize all his work, including the brilliant landscapes.

For just as *The Street* is conscious of being a displacement of a forest (with all its allusions to wood and the mythology of woods), so *The Passage* is conscious of being where a meadow once was. The dog is sheeplike, a man carries bread, and we are only a few streets from Saint-Germain-des-Prés, of the Meadows).

Inside the painting's mysteriousness there had been all along a familiarity I had not isolated until I stood before the canvas itself. A more wonderful way of seeing Proust's theory of the redemption of time in triumphant proof I cannot imagine.

Another surprise was to notice that for all the resonances in this most Balthusian of all Balthus's work (the Rilkean question, as of the Saltimbanques, "Who are these people?"; its kinship to Beckett and Sartre), it belongs with a rightness to the Paris of Simenon. There's the same flat ordinariness, as if to say: Look, the world is not really a mystery at all. It appears to be, but look again. These eight people, a dog, and a doll are the very essence of a Left Bank back street. The fine strangeness of it all is in our minds. The old woman with her cane, a concierge nipping out briefly to do her shopping, can tell you all about these people. She is the kind of spiteful old soul who gives Maigret and Janvier their best information. Our seeing the painting is very like Maigret's learning a neighborhood where a crime has been committed.

The figure we see from the back (a self-portrait, according to Jean Leymarie), who is coming from the baker's, is a standard type in the *quartier.* Maigret would suspect him of all manner of irresponsibility, bohemian attitudes, and cosmopolitan vices.

The man on the left, resettling his trousers, and the aging dwarf on the right are standard Simenon characters. They also belong to Beckett, a denizen of this street, whose *Molly* and *En attendant Godot* are contemporary with the painting in the Spenglerian and literal sense.

These gnomish creatures, the most accessible of Balthus's enigmas, are not satiric, symbolic, or archetypical. They are simply misshapen bodies for which Balthus makes a place in order to chasten his (and our) voluptuous taste for the world. Apollo is dull without Hobgoblin.

24

BALTHUS'S EARLIER cityscape *The Street* (1933) states with
more theatricality the theme of *The Passage du Commerce
Saint-André*: that pedestrians on a street are preoccupied,
sealed within themselves, without cognizance of each
other. Each painting, *The Street* and *The Passage,* insists
that the eye that's awake in all this sleep of attention
is the artist's, making a basic definition, sweetly obvi-
ous but extraordinarily important, of what a painting
is in the most archaic meaning of image, the *seen.*

25

WE HAVE adequate, if not accurate, reasons for the visual fields of all the epochs of graphic mimesis except the earliest and the latest. We feel confident that a Hogarth or a Goya exists in a history, an iconographic tradition, an anthropology that we can successfully examine. We do not have this confidence with prehistoric cave murals or with Balthus. We are as uncertain of Archilochus's exact meaning as of Beckett and Joyce. One pattern of meaning is lost, the other has chosen to move outside our received structure of references, to enlarge it.

In the two street paintings there is first of all a sense of absurd tragedy in the discreteness of the characters. Two adolescents, a boy and a girl, struggle playfully in *The Street,* unaware that they look like a rape, perhaps wholly unaware of the emotional forces disguised in their play. They are like the adolescents in the roomscapes who take poses that are erotically suggestive, ambiguous, tentative of symbolism. There's the same vagueness of purposelessness in Cocteau and Proust: the love scenes between Marcel and Albertine are all purest Balthus.

These adolescents are like kittens enjoying themselves immensely at a game of disemboweling each other. Their claws are retracted; we are fairly certain that they don't know what they are doing, though nature does. What does nature know about Balthus's pedestrians on a street?

Adolescents play at sex, a cook strolls on the sidewalk (if we don't know that he's a signboard for the menu), a little girl plays with a racquet and ball, a boy walks with a gesture like a bandleader's at the head of a parade, his face rapt with inner attention and Whittingtonian aspiration. A well-dressed woman steps onto the curb, seemingly in a reverie (is she gesturing to her child in the nurse's arms ahead?), a nursemaid in an apron carries a child wearing a sailor suit and reading a handbill, as awkwardly posed as a ventriloquist's dummy. There is something of Oskar Schlemmer's lay-figure poise and plumb-line balance to them.

Indeed, if we were told that we are looking at puppets, our eye immediately supplies their strings by noticing all the perpendicular lines directly above heads, wrists, and ankles that might be puppet strings visible for sections of their length: a metaphysical idea.

We remember Rilke's symbolism of puppet and angel in the *Duino Elegies,* the empty and the full, the fated and fate itself, and remember the iconography of the doll, straw man, and puppet in de Chirico, Eliot, Pound, Yeats, *Petrouchka,* Karel Čapek, Jarry, Carrà, Ensor, Wyndham Lewis.

These sentient puppets inhabit two simultaneous worlds: they yearn (inchoate yearning applies as subject to a good half of Balthus's work) and they are "tossed and wrung" (as Rilke says in the Fifth Elegy) by fate, like the figures in Picasso's Blue and Rose periods.

26

If BALTHUS's figure paintings are all purgatorial in the sense that brooding, looking inward, abiding patiently for things to come are modes of existential suffering, his landscapes are visions of paradise. Where the landscapes have figures, they are active and jubilant.

27

A work of art, like a foreign language, is closed to us until we learn how to read it. Meaning is latent, seemingly hidden. There is also the illusion that the meaning is concealed. A work of art is a structure of signs, each meaningful. It follows that a work of art has one meaning only. For an explicator to blur an artist's meaning, or to be blind to his achievement, is a kind of treason, a betrayal. The arrogance of insisting that a work of art means what you think it means is a mistake that closes off curiosity, perception, the adventure of discovery.

28

IN CURVED Einsteinian space we are at all times, technically, looking at the back of our own head. (There's *mich,* me, in with *Marx* and *fox* and *moose* in the *Mookse* of Joyce's "Eins within a space and a wearywide space it wast ere wohned a Mookse"). In *The Passage du Commerce Saint-André* and again in *The Painter and His Model* Balthus has portrayed himself from the back. Fourteen of the thirty-five drawings of himself in *Mitsou* are from the back.

Sᴇɴsᴜᴏᴜs ᴄʟᴀʀɪᴛʏ, children in the old-fashioned smocks of a France only recently folded into history forever, high-ceilinged rooms, Parisian streets, châteaux, farms, meadows: Balthus's accomplished realism turns out on inspection to be both a lyric vision and a complex enigma. *Ainigma,* Greek for "riddle." In the Old Testament it means something terrible, defying understanding; Paul uses it in "For now we see through a glass darkly: but then face to face . . ." (I Corinthians 13:12). "Darkly" is *en ainigmati,* as in a dark, puzzling, riddling saying: Paul is alluding to oracles, sibylline sayings.

Balthus is enigmatic in several masterly paintings. Of *The Street* (1933), we would like to know if we are looking at Surrealism, an old-fashioned allegory, a riddle, or a deployment of symbols. We turn to critics for help. Here's Jean Leymarie:

> The white-clad carpenter carrying a beam as golden-hued as the mystic wood is the axis of pure form and auburn light around which gravitate the other figures, a prey to their phantasms or sunk in their dreams: the pair of schoolboys caught at their little game; the cataleptic baker under his big white cap; the dreamy girl chasing a red ball that punctuates

the grey street; the workman with a cap whose firm step and strange face come as a surprise; the two women in black, seen from behind, one with her feet jutting out on the sidewalk, the other holding her sleeping child in her arms like a puppet.

(Leymarie, 9)

This description is surely the product of a passing glance. The "pair of schoolboys" are a fresh boy and a girl whose skirt he is lifting (in an earlier version, bowdlerized by the painter himself, the boy was groping the girl's genitals). The "cataleptic baker" is a wooden sign on which menus are posted (Rewald, 60). One of the women in black is stepping up onto the sidewalk ("feet jutting out" may be static in the translation), and the "sleeping child" of the other is reading a piece of paper. As for the "beam" (more translator's static?), it is a plank, and probably a signboard, and the figure's clothes are more likely those of a painter than a carpenter.

The amorous boy and girl suggest an Ovidian episode, perhaps an Apollo and Daphne. If Lévi-Strauss were to begin a structural analysis of *The Street* with this perception, he would then connect the little girl playing with a red ball with Peitho, Eros's sister. As we know from Anacreon, a red ball preceded Eros's bow and arrows as his inflaming instrument. Wood, Daphne's transformation, appears immediately as the wooden restaurant sign (easily mistaken, and in another reading of the painting, to be taken for a real cook). Then what?

Or Lévi-Strauss might take another tack: we have puppy love at one extreme, a nurse or mother with a child at the other. In between, childhood at play, and two professions (cooking and carpentry). We can read the woman stepping onto the curb as the mother of the child in its nurse's arms.

All of this keeps suggesting an allegory.

If we see the boy and girl as an allusion to a classical erotic pursuit, a good candidate for the allusion is the grasping of a nymph by Zephyrus in Botticelli's *Primavera.*

Indeed, if we put the one painting over the other, with Botticelli reversed, we discover that the nine figures in the one correspond to each of the nine in the other: Cupid (corresponding to Balthus's Peitho with the red ball), Mercury (corresponding to Balthus's messenger boy), Venus (who in gesture is like Balthus's woman in black stepping onto the sidewalk), Flora, a nymph, Zephyrus, and the three Graces.

Now the iconographic enigmas start to do all sorts of witty things. The Graces are Aglaia (Splendor), who presided over victories at the games (is she our tot with the racquet and ball?); Euphrosyne (Mirth), who presided over good spirits and happiness (our marching messenger boy?); and Thalia (Abundance), who presided over festivals and feasts and later became the muse of comedy (our wooden cook?).

These three figures make a zigzag among the others, like the sidewalk on the left.

Globe and circles at the top of the painting correspond to Botticelli's grove of golden apples.

A street is the traditional stage for comedy. *The Street* seems to have absorbed comic motifs from Plautus to Hogarth. (The restaurant sign, a saint with a cup, is Hogarthian.)

In Christian iconography the three Graces become Faith, Hope, and Charity. If we continue the singular line between the outermost and the next red stripe on the bistro awning at the right, we discover that it ends exactly at the painting's bottom left corner. The resulting triangle encloses a woman with a red cross on her hat (Faith), an aspiring and confident messenger boy (Hope), and a nurse carrying a child (Charity).

Note how the man carrying the plank (which several critics have read as Christ with the cross) divides the composition into two groups, each of which contain a child, youths, and adults.

The child being carried is reading, myopically, out of the side of his eyes. So are we, in all this speculation. So are we.

30

LIKE HIS childhood mentor Rilke in the Fifth Duino Elegy, Balthus asks in his studies of so many adolescents who we are in our cycle of budding, blossoming, falling to seed again *"in diesem mühsamen Nirgends."* Our "never-contented will" pitches us like acrobats even in boredom and contemplative repose. Rilke was meditating on Picasso's *Les Saltimbanques,* and Picasso's gesture in buying and leaving Balthus's *The Children* (1937) to the Louvre as part of the Donation Picasso seems a deliberate return of Rilke's homage,* thereby defining the kinship of three symbols of *Dastehn,* the existential *thereness*—the Saltimbanques, from which came the Fifth Elegy, from which came *The Children* of Balthus.

---

* The Children now hangs in the Musée Picasso.

31

ANOTHER WORK, indeed, in time an oeuvre, that came from *Les Saltimbanques,* is the earliest surviving story of Eudora Welty, "Acrobats in a Park." This story, written "in, or about, the year 1935," was turned up in the Mississippi Department of Archives and History in 1967 by Kenneth Graham of the University of Sheffield, who published it in *Delta,* a journal published at the Université Paul Valéry in Montpellier. It was again published at Clemson, with an introduction by Jan Nordby Gretlund, a Danish scholar of American writing. The story is a kind of translation of Picasso's figures into a family of itinerant acrobats. Welty makes them part of a circus performing in her native Jackson. In an introduction to the story in 1980 she wrote:

> Under the guidance of instinct, I made the acrobats into a *family,* and set them down on the ground in Smith Park in Jackson. . . . In performance, their act had been the feat of erecting a structure of their bodies that held together and stood like a wall. When I was writing about the family act, I was writing about the family itself, its strength as a unit and its frailty under stress. . . .
>
> What strikes me now, and what I was

unaware of then, was that these acrobats were prophesying for the subject that would concern me most in all my work lying ahead. From points of view within and without, I've been writing about this Wall ever since and what happens to it. Indeed, in this story are the beginnings of the subject in its double form: the solid unity of the family thinking itself unassailable, and the outsiders who would give much to enter it—most often out of love and with the effect, sometimes, of liberation.

(Welty, iv)

32

Picasso liked to paint his own children in the costumes of the acrobats of the Blue and Rose periods, to emphasize that the vulnerable and wan people he painted then were indeed families (and how many Holy Families he has slipped into his circus people, only half disguised) and that their coherence was as frail as Eudora Welty intuited.

Balthus has painted some of his most hauntingly impressive portraits of fathers and daughters, of families, of husbands and wives, though it is the daughters on whom his fame rests.

33

Balthus's adolescents are Rilke's "bees of the invisible," taking in from books, from daydreaming, from an as yet ambiguous longing, from staring out windows at trees, sustenances that will be available in time as Proustian ripenesses, necessities of the heart.

Ultimately it is Balthus's sensibility that gives his canvases their distinction, the quality of his attention, the unlikely subtlety and boldness of his sensuality, the harmony he creates of tensions, inarticulatenesses, ambiguities, volume, light, elusive moments.

34

As SAUSSURE could not, or would not, define language, so we should not define art, which may be a granary door in Ogol or Brancusi's *The Kiss,* a film or a Mycenaean shield. Nature without art is signless and brutal, but "real"—and here reality means survival tactics (feral caution, stalking, fleeing, mating, abiding, identifying a territory in which somebody else, not us, is the stranger). Culture, having art for sign, is symbol, rite, custom, and is "unreal." Is the dividing line between nature and culture the imagination? From which invention, language, number, proportion, manners. Is misbehavior a recourse to nature, or a malfunction of culture, or simply a breach of the ethical code with which we control nature and ourselves in a society? Culture and its ground, agriculture, are the prime Balthusian assertions. His largest theme may be the care a culture has for its young.

35

BALTHUS'S PAINTINGS are illustrations for a writer we can imagine the style of, but who doesn't exist. This writer would have Francis Ponge's metaphysical sense of French meadows, Proust's sensuality of girl's bodies and clothes, Rilke's ripeness of fate and time. But what writer can deal with the happy fat boy and his pigeons, the Japanese woman in her Turkish room, the crones and gnomes, the daimon cats, part Cheshire, part hearth-god?

36

The large glass fruit dish on a silver base which a baby is trying to reach in *The Greedy Child* (1938) appears again in *Still Life with a Figure* (1940). In the former it contains peaches and plums; in the latter, apples. Sabine Rewald gives the title of *Still Life with a Figure* as *Le goûter*, "The Snack." A taste, a between-meals meal, is the sense of *goûter*, and the word comes from *gustare*, to be pleased by taste. Our word *choose* derives from the same root.

Apples, wine (or cider), bread with a knife left in it mid-slice. A girl looks at it all, one hand on the table, the other against a large tapestry, or curtain. This cloth is lifted so that its largest fold has a depression resembling an adolescent vagina. The appearance of such a drawn-back curtain in Christian iconography "signifies the revelation of a sacred space" (Rewald, 100). The still life, except for the apples, is eucharistic; the bread and wine of the mass persist in still life, and began before Christianity in the painted meals (to sustain the dead) in Egyptian tombs as well as in Old Testament imagery (Amos's "basket of summer fruit" symbolizing God's bounty).

The apple comes late in Balthus. It is not used insistently or programmatically as a symbol of the Fall; it is an adjective not a verb. It occurs in paintings that meditate on the transition from girl to woman. They occur in the same glass bowl in *The Living Room* (1943), where a rite of passage is depicted: a dreaming girl on a sofa, a girl kneeling on the floor and reading. There's a score open on the piano; the tablecloth (analogue of skirt) has been pushed back to reveal part of the tabletop. The red apples say that Balthus thinks of maturity in Judeo-Christian terms: a fall, a *felix culpa*. In Fourier's Harmony the Little Bands and Little Hordes of children will think of their older members who have begun sexual experiences as fallen angels.

A basket of apples sits on the floor in *The Three Sisters*.

The trees in *The Triangular Field* are apple.

The orange in *The Golden Fruit* (the golden apples of mythology were probably oranges) and the unidentifiable fruit in *The Turkish Room* (surely not eggs, as Rewald says) serve the symbolic function of apples.

In Christian iconography, a pear symbolizes the Redemption, and apple and pear are frequently together in Madonnas, Mary being the redemption of Eve, Christ of Adam.

In the eloquent *Painter and His Model* of 1981, in which Balthus is opening the curtains of his studio (rhyming with the gnomish figure opening the drapes in *The Room*) and the model, fully dressed, is kneeling at a chair and looking at a drawing (rhyming with many kneeling, reading girls), the tabletop still life is of a box of biscuits (wheat field, meadow) and two apples and a pear, triumphantly together for the first time in Balthus's work. There is also a ladder in this culminating painting: traditional symbol of spiritual climbing.

37

EIGHTEENTH-CENTURY satire became nineteenth-century observation. In the twentieth century observation became surreal. It became an ironic sensuality, and the basis for satire, which was once moral, became irony. As if by attraction, or even kinship, observation, along with its concerns for sentiment and social justice, followed satire to sit on its new ironic base. Thus Surrealism in the hands of Max Ernst or R. B. Kitaj became a classical mode of the century and reinforced the century's characterization of reality as an enigma. "The great Surrealists, for me," Kitaj has remarked, "are not the orthodox Surrealists, who are generally lesser artists, but people like Picasso, Bacon, Balthus" (Livingstone, 42).

The master figures at the heart of Surrealism, Ernst, Chagall, and de Chirico, have made a metaphysical poetry of modern painting, moving between the extremes of the collage to the fantasy of folktale or dream.

Balthus's space in all this may well be outside Surrealism altogether, while enjoying diplomatic relations. Kitaj's parody of, or conversation with, *The Street*—his *Cecil Court, London WC2 (The Refugees)* of 1984—is more a spoof than a sustained parody. Its stretched Chagallian figure and allusions to private associations show the likenesses and differences of the two painters. Balthus's subjectivity is absorbed completely; Kitaj's is allowed to remain on the surface, to create a turbulence where Balthus insists upon a calm.

38

ONE BECOMES inured to the hard truth that reality is a function of dreams, that things are perceived according to what they symbolize, which is what caused them to be selected in the first place from myriads of others, all competing for attention. Symbolism is the language of dreams (Zolla, 16).

39

Baudelaire, in *The Salon of 1846*: "Many times, when faced with these countless samples of the universal feeling [erotic drawings], I have found myself wishing that the poet, the connoisseur and the philosopher could grant themselves the enjoyment of a Museum of Love, where there would be a place for everything from St. Teresa's undirected affections down to the serious debauches of the ages of ennui. No doubt an immense distance separates *Le Départ pour l'île de Cythère* from the miserable daubs which hang above a cracked pot and a rickety side-table in a harlot's room; but with a subject of such importance, nothing should be neglected. Besides, all things are sanctified by genius, and if these subjects were treated with the necessary care and reflection, they would in no wise be soiled by that revolting obscenity, which is bravado rather than truth" (Baudelaire, 71).

1

2

3

4

5

6

7

40

STANISLAS KLOSSOWSKI de Rola protests in an introduction to a book of his father's paintings that "the fabled theme of the young adolescent girl, which Balthus has treated repeatedly, has nothing whatever to do with sexual obsession except perhaps in the eye of the beholder" (Klossowski de Rola, 9). This is ingenuous, and fair enough, but what's being said here? Whatever I might know about the artist's obsessions (which in my case is nothing), that knowledge would remain irrelevant, and the paintings would remain unchanged.

"These girls," he continues, "are in fact emblematic archetypes belonging to another, higher realm." This assertion is unfair to Balthus's penetration into privileged female space, rivaled only by Vermeer and Degas. So human and valuable an understanding should not be diminished by Neoplatonic Jungian jargon. Balthus's girls are sexy, charming French adolescents painted with a fresh reseeing of the human body, with humor, with wit, with clarity, and with an innocence that we can locate in adolescent idealism itself rather than in an obsession.

The young body has not yet accepted the permanent mask of clothing, as the faces of the young are not yet masks. It seems to me wrong to see a philosophical abstraction when the artist has given us flesh and blood, a perfection of tone and moment, a magic stillness of time, accurate perceptions of moods which few painters or poets can equal.

Young Girl at a Window (1955)—a girl with her left leg resting on a chair, her arms on a windowsill, seen from behind, looking out on boughs, bushes, a barn—defines so well the pensive quiet of the moment that archetypes and emblems add nothing to the painting's beauty or its success. The girl is civilized, the house bespeaks a culture, as do the barn and the trees. Balthus is indeed painting adolescence but, more important, adolescence in this particular French place. Subject and symbol are fused inextricably. Great art is always eloquently tautological; the world in Balthus is a metaphor of itself.

41

In the Wittgensteinian convergence where *Ethik und Aes-thetik sind Eins* we can locate a subsistent morality far more cogent for Balthus than Stanislas Klossowski de Rola's "higher realm" of archetypes. Centuries before Plato beauty was a kind of good, and the appreciation of it a pleasure. Beauty has also traditionally been an outward sign of the soul's beauty. Balthus integrates this ancient tradition with Darwinian naturalism (beauty as sexual attraction). Darwin suspected that there was always "something left over" after sexual attractiveness has done its work, and that this something was what we call beauty, and that it may have given rise to art. The grace of line in a Lascaux horse is not the horse, but something that has been abstracted from it.

The puritanical objections leveled at Balthus are fueled by prurience equating candor with misplaced desire. The objection to desire is not moral but economic. A woman's body is marketable; its sexuality is not to be recognized in any but an economic context.

42

APPLE IS both discord and harmony. Pear is concord, sweetness, harvest bounty. Eve's *malum,* meaning "evil" and "apple"; and there's the resemblance of glans penis to an apple). Theocritus VII: Eros compared to a red apple, Philinos (the beloved) to the mellow ripeness of a pear.

Pear: Castor and Pollux, friendship of teacher and pupil, artist and model. Leda's egg: apple (Helen) and pear (the Dioskouroi).

Apple and pear in Balthus's *The Painter and His Model* are a symbol (however we arrive at it through the Greek, Roman, and Christian grammar of the erotic apple and the friendly pear) of the bonding of artist and model.

The artist is opening the curtain at the window, as the dwarfish gnome does in *The Room.* Tasks assigned to goblins from the underworld thirty years before are now the duty of the artist himself. Is this a discovery that the dark of intuition is always illuminated by the process of creation? This is a good example of what Freud seems to have meant when he said that the *it* of the subconscious can be the catalyst of the integrated, wise self. The troll under the mountain emerges with the gold. There's a ladder in the painting, symbol of ascent.

Art in the twentieth century is best characterized by its redemption of time in its own terms. Picasso's final meditation on the erotic agony of the flesh, his *347 Gravures,* has for its final plate a meadow before a wood, and a serene artist and model. Kafka's last story is set in a meadow, and is a fable about the powers of the artist.

43

IT IS precisely those harmonies which have become dis-
sonant we want to study in every way we can, for they
had a harmonic origin. They changed. We changed. We
need to know why.

44

BALTHUS, LIKE Kafka, is a master of gesture and posture. For Kafka the body was a semaphore transmitting a language we cannot read. Balthus's gestures also defy interpretation. The luxuriant stretch, ecstatic comfort, looks out of the side of the eyes—these reserve meaning that would be apparent in Goya and Hogarth. They are Kafka's existential kinetics.

45

A THEATER of silence. A film about Balthus (Fellini has considered making one) would want César Franck or Mozart for its soundtrack. The voice-over might plausibly be the First and Fifth Duino Elegies, Ponge's "The Meadow," Proust, Gertrude Stein.

46

WHEN WE place Balthus beside the intimist painting of Denmark, especially Købke and Hammershøi, with whom he would seem to have a similar feeling for interior space and for landscape, we see instead his philosophical difference. There is an awesome existential bareness in Balthus. He is not, however, a nihilist like Nabokov, rejecting all humanism along with humanity itself. He is closer to Beckett and Ionesco than to Sartre. There is the ungiving understanding that what's of value in life is inherited from the past. In the present we have healthy bodies and their fate, nothing else. Our century's events do not exist in Balthus. His portraits are of artists and friends. The canvases done during the Second World War are of farm life and girls in provincial houses.

47

IF SURREALISM tried to find a European subconscious mind that is kin in irrationality and mythic structure to primitive cultures (it has been noticed that French ethnology and Surrealism have mutualities and affinities), Balthus has worked not with spiritual substrata where civilization and barbarity have common roots, but with the high surfaces of civilization (the ancient farm, the studio, well-furnished rooms, the streets of Paris). A commentary on any of the paintings will extend deep into history, biography, and rich iconographic detail.

48

BALTHUS'S AWKWARDNESSES, as in the early paintings and the Brontë drawings and later in sporadic passages, are deliberate. They happen well after he had achieved a sophisticated style. They are like Beckett's writing in French because he felt that his English was too facile. Balthus's use of rough surfaces in his Roman period served the same purpose: to humble facileness.

In these awkwardnesses we see a kinship with Henri Rousseau, who in many ways is Balthus's secret master. Compare *The Poet and His Muse* with the portrait of Derain. Each eludes the neoclassical in its own way.

49

In the course of an essay praising the painting of Anita Albus, Claude Lévi-Strauss makes this observation: "The history of contemporary painting, as it has developed during the last hundred years, is confronted with a paradox. Painters have come to reject the subject in favor of what is now called, with revealing discretion, their 'work' [*travail*]; one would not be so bold as to speak of 'craft' [*métier*]. On the other hand, only if one continued to see in painting a means of knowledge [*un moyen de connaissance*]—that of a whole outside the artist's work—would a craftsmanship inherited from the old masters regain its importance and keep its place as an object of study and reflection" (Lévi-Strauss, 256).

Lévi-Strauss ends each of his four volumes of *Mythologies* with a critique of the confusion into which art, philosophy, and civilization itself have fallen. Music has lost its harmony, literature its resolving plot, painting its skill in interpreting the world. In abandoning a discipline of the self (Michel Foucault's last subject), we have reversed the deference to nature in which civilization began. We must move away from Sartre's "Hell is other people." The crux is this: that instead of asking the world not to threaten our solitude, our personal and solipsistic order, we should so behave ourselves as not to threaten the world's order. This involves our understanding, and agreeing to, the world's order, a process of complex immensity, but one in which culturally the arts have a great, mediating, role.

Lévi-Strauss allows Max Ernst and Anita Albus the distinction of being true artists. We can, without violence to his strict demands, include Balthus, along with others. If the artist imparts and structures a knowledge of the world, he must speak so individually and with such fresh insight that his work extends rather than duplicates knowledge. He must give us new eyes. He must educate our sensibility.

In time, we will see Balthus as kin to Joyce on the one hand (our biological mandate civilized by a poetry of desire and its constraints), and to Proust on the other (the tragedy of time illuminated by the beauty and wonder of being alive).

50

WHAT IS Balthus? The Blue and Rose periods in color and translated from Montmartre to the Faubourgs Saint-Germain and Saint-Honoré, to châteaux in the Rhone Valley? Courbet in the age of Rilke and Cocteau? He is, most certainly, the artist whose vision of the French spirit will increase in subtlety and radiance.

51

HENRY DE Montherlant, that stoic and sensualist whom
fate dropped into the France of our time rather than
into the Roman consular service of the second century
where he belonged, answered a critic's query as to "the
great men who had influenced him most" by naming
Pyrrhon of Elis, Anacreon, and Regulus, *"le Sceptique, le
Voluptueux, le Héros."* He added that their influence was
a single force. "Do not consider any one of them without the other two." It is doubtful that the Pyrrhon we
know about resembles with any accuracy the philosopher of that name; Regulus is certainly a myth; and we
wonder which Anacreon Montherlant had in mind, the
anonymous author (or authors) of the Alexandrine imi-
tations, or the poet whose work survives in such muti-
lated form that we can only guess what it was when
whole? Balthus might answer the question with Rilke,
Courbet, Proust; or Emily Brontë, Vermeer, Colette.
We would be cautioned, as by Montherlant, that the
influence is an integration of forces. And Balthus is rich
in *hommages*: a still life bows to Morandi, a hand holding
a mirror to Utamaro, a cat to Hogarth.

52

Balthus, like Daumier, allows caricature beside traditional academic rendering. So does nature. Velázquez's dwarves and midgets serve to place an infanta or king in the chain of being as his society understood it. There is a profounder meaning to Balthus's ogres: they belong with the voluptuousness of his girls, for sex, when it comes, will be goblin as much as it will be Eros. Priapus is a homely and earthy god. Look at the goblin in Fuseli's *Nightmare*.

53

BALTHUS WORKS in an imaginary space between interior and exterior worlds. What we see in his paintings is not what a photograph would record: certain cats and human figures would be missing. The man laying the fire in *The Golden Days* may well exist only in the imagination of the girl studying her face in a mirror. In *The Room* we can plausibly read the painting as having one figure only. The stunted woman may be imagining the luxuriating girl. The strolling "cook" in *The Street* is a flat restaurant sign. Is the walking figure in *The Dream* a dream?

54

PICASSO PAINTED in the Latin of the Principate, when portraiture became big-eyed and staring, the human form became stiff and heavy, and the world was fascinated by but weary of violence. Braque painted in Greek. Balthus paints in the patrician French of Henry de Montherlant, aloof from vulgarity.

55

Mitsou IS contemporary with Rilke's *Sonnets to Orpheus,*
and is itself a version of the Orpheus myth.

56

OCTAVIO PAZ ends a poem dedicated to Balthus with *"La luz es tiempo que se piensa"* ("Light is time thinking about itself," Eliot Weinberger translates; Paz, 95). "La vista, el tacto" ("Sight, Touch") meditates on the tactile abilities of eyesight, on light's sculpting matter, so that we see it according to the strategies of light on objects. In modern painting we have two traditions of light. One analyzes light as a vibrant rain. From Pissarro and Cézanne to Seurat and Signac we see the physics of color, the dance and ricochet of the photon, a granulation into discrete particles.

The other tradition ranges from the blind fingers of Picasso to Balthus's treatment of light as a transparent solid in which matter is submerged. Heraclitean fire, the one; Aristotelian solidity, the other. In Monet light visits the haystack; in Balthus light embraces, fuses, clings.

57

A CULTURE's sense of the erotic is a dialect, often exclusively parochial, as native to it as its sense of humor and its cooking. Sexuality being a biological imperative, we imagine that we comprehend Manet, Fragonard, and Watteau when their subjects are erotic; Goya, Rubens, and Rembrandt; Greek, Japanese, and Dogon erotic art. Each culture has its taboos, its lines drawn between decency and the obscene. These can be absurd, prudish, religious, bourgeois, legal demarcations. Because they are proscriptive, causes of anxiety, shame, and salacious humor, these cultural decisions about sexuality become richly symbolic.

The nearer an artist works to the erotic politics of his own culture, the more he gets its concerned attention. Gauguin's naked Polynesian girls, brown and remote, escape the scandal of Balthus's, although a Martian observer could not see the distinction.

58

TEXTILES WITH floral designs are indoor meadows in Balthus. As the meadow itself is his prime symbol of nature and the pubescent female body his symbol of spirit integral with matter, the two together are his *signum mundi*. The Turkish or Persian carpet is in fact a token meadow, the floor of the Arab tent, prayer rug, dining space, bed. Northern Europeans used these beautiful carpets as table covers and wall hangings, as we can see in Holbein. Meadow and pasture in the Old Testament become the ground for Jesus' pastoral images, and in Greek poetry as early as Sappho and Archilochus the erotic affinity between meadow and girl which will persist through medieval and Renaissance art (in the Provençal poets, Petrarch, Chaucer, Shakespeare) is already a mature convention. We find in the Cologne fragment of Archilochus:

> I said no more, but took her hand,
> Laid her down in a thousand flowers,
> And put my soft wool cloak around her.
>
> I slid my arm under her neck
> To still the fear in her eyes,
> For she was trembling like a fawn,

Touched her warm breasts with light fingers,
Straddled her neatly and pressed
Against her fine, hard, bared crotch.

Sappho, imagining a girl who is now grown and a wife in Sardis:

And now she moves among the Lydian ladies
As when the sun has set and the stars come out
And the rose-red moon

Lifts into the midst of their pale brightness.
Her light is everywhere, on the salt-bitter sea,
On fields thick and rich with flowers
And beautiful under dew,

On roses, tangled parsley, and the honey-headed clover.
Her light is everywhere, remembering
Atthis in her young sweetness, desiring her
With tender, heavy heart.

In *The Toilette* (1957) Balthus has placed a standing adolescent, nude save for white knee socks and red slippers, before a bed with a flowery eiderdown. *The Cup of Coffee* (1960), an essay about its motif, meditating on its descent from the odalisques of Delacroix and Ingres through Matisse, places a girl in an arabesque of carpets and floral textiles. *The Turkish Room* (1966), *The Three Sisters* (1965), *Sleeping Nude* (1980) also deploy girls on a ground of meadowy carpets.

59

CHARDIN PAINTED in an age of conversation, Rembrandt in one of argument and disputation: both depict objects found in darkness by a remote light. Chardin's light is mellow, kind, sweet. In Rembrandt light hallows what it illumines while it fights the darkness. Chardin's light is reason; Rembrandt's, faith and revelation. Balthus's light is a plenum, as thorough, pedantic, and secular as a page of Sartre.

60

EAKINS AND Balthus. Their differences are many: Eakins
has none of Balthus's irony, wit, or comedy. Their
sensuality, surprisingly, brings them together, for
both insist that the body has a mind, and that its in-
tellectual, speculative, thinking life is integral to the
sensuous life of the body. They share a candor ex-
pressed in exactitude and honesty. Eakins shared
Whitman's vision of the erotic, and painted wrestlers
as intimately entwined as lovers, and male swimmers
as comradely as in an Athenian gymnasium fre-
quented by Alcibiades. All of Eakins's work is of
thinking, skilled, accomplished people: mathemati-
cians, athletes, poets. Eakins painted the arrived;
Balthus, becoming. Both explored private, privileged
space, with nudity as the occasion for their tact.

61

IN WANTING the modern Olympics to include children, to be played in the nude, and for there to be no spectators, Coubertin showed a hopeless ignorance of what the world outside his study had become. Children were an Arnoldian (as well as a classical) touch: the green playing fields of England, where the cricketers and ballplayers could read Thucydides in Greek, Horace in Latin, Ronsard in French. The nudity was from the ancient games themselves, and the banishment of spectators his aristocrat's distrust of a crowd's idle curiosity. Spectators smacked of the drunken, vicious dandies who watched boxing and cockfights in a morbid pursuit of excitement. Spectators were ignorant of sport, devoid of idealism, and avid merely to be amused. But Coubertin seemed to have no notion that sport in modern times would be precisely the Circus Maximus all over again, with the crowd hoping to see the athlete break his neck, the racing-car driver die in burning gasoline, soccer teams brawling.

Balthus disappoints many expectations by being from Coubertin's deployment of values. He is never vulgar, never paints in the vernacular. And his idealism is as vulnerable as Coubertin's to journalistic acid and public opinion.

62

"WHEN HE was nineteen years old Picasso came to Paris, that was in 1900, into a world of painters who had completely learned everything they could from seeing at what they were looking. From Seurat to Courbet they were all of them looking with their eyes and Seurat's eyes then began to tremble at what his eyes were seeing, he commenced to doubt if in looking he could see" (Stein, 1). ("Seeing at what they were looking" for "looking at what they were seeing" and "from Seurat to Courbet" for "from Courbet to Seurat" are Steinian games with *our* eyes.) Balthus's eyes have never doubted. The decisiveness and radiant clarity of his landscapes were achieved in faith, loyalty, and reverence. They are a rebeginning after Impressionism, and have learned from it.

63

BASIL BUNTING, the Northumberland poet, found another reason to damn the shallowness and ignorance of our times in that he had reached a great age before he saw the painting of Balthus. Yeats was luckier. Federico Fellini, writing about Balthus in awe and reverence, calls him the master custodian of our heritage in painting (Leymarie and Fellini, 17). Balthus was admired and collected by Picasso and Albert Camus, yet American critics with a few exceptions have denounced him for both his subject matter and his style. He inspires in them a hysterical prudery that has taken such diverse forms as attacking him as a pornographer and as being a false claimant to his Polish title.

64

The Passage du Commerce Saint-André is in conversation with *La Grande Jatte.* With Jules Laforgue as an interpreter, if La Belle Époque can't quite believe postwar Paris in the 1940s. Both paintings comment on the Revolution. French dialogues with the past are distant or close: Roland Barthes might have been one of Gide's sensitive adolescents. Poulenc converses with Machaut, Picasso with Poussin, Braque with Chardin. Balthus goes back to Balzac, for whom reality was magnificent in its monstrous ugliness, for whom youth was at once silly and beautiful.

Both paintings depict a Sunday. The old woman in the *Passage* will have lived through the two intervening world wars.

Works Cited

Baudelaire, Charles, *The Mirror of Art: Critical Studies,* tr. and ed. Jonathan Mayne. New York: Phaidon, 1955.

Colette, *Mitsou,* tr. Raymond Postgate, in *Six Novels by Colette.* New York: Modern Library, 1957.

Comfort, Alex, *Darwin and the Naked Lady: Discursive Essays on Biology and Art.* New York: George Braziller, 1961.

Dobyns, Stephen, *The Balthus Poems.* New York: Atheneum, 1982.

Klossowski de Rola, Stanislas, *Balthus.* New York: Harper & Row, 1983.

Lévi-Strauss, Claude, *The Elementary Structures of Kinship,* tr. James Harle Bell, John Richard Sturmer, and Rodney Needham. Boston: Beacon Press, 1969.

———, *The View from Afar,* tr. Joachim Neugroschel and Phoebe Hoss. New York: Basic Books, 1985.

Leymarie, Jean, *Balthus.* Geneva: Skira, 1979.

———, and Federico Fellini, *Balthus.* Venice: Edizioni La Biennale, 1980.

Lifton, Betty Jean, *The King of Children: A Biography of Janusc Korczak.* New York: Farrar, Straus & Giroux, 1988.

Livingstone, Marco, *R. B. Kitaj.* New York: Rizzoli, 1985.

Merleau-Ponty, Maurice, *The Primacy of Perception,* ed. James M. Edie. Chicago: Northwestern University Press, 1964.

Paz, Octavio, *A Tree Within,* tr. Eliot Weinberger. New York: New Directions, 1988.

Rewald, Sabine, *Balthus.* New York: The Metropolitan Museum of Art and Harry N. Abrams, 1984.

Schapiro, Meyer, *Modern Art.* New York: George Braziller, 1978.

Smith, Gary, ed., *On Walter Benjamin: Critical Essays and Recollections.* Cambridge, MA, and London: MIT Press, 1988.

Stein, Gertrude, *Picasso.* London: B. T. Batsford, 1938.

Welty, Eudora, *Acrobats in a Park.* Northridge, CA: Lord John Press, 1980.

Zolla, Elémire, *Archetypes.* London: George Allen & Unwin, 1981.